DANDELION

ADVENTURES

by L.
Patricia Kite

illustrated
by Anca
Hariton

THE MILLBROOK
PRESS, INC.
BROOKFIELD,
CONNECTICUT

To my brilliant and charming sister, Michelle Padams Brant,
author of Timeless Walks in San Francisco.   L.P.K.

For my family of friends who can see strength
and beauty in a weed, and for Peter.   A.H.

Library of Congress Cataloging-in-Publication Data
Kite, L. Patricia.
Dandelion adventures / by L. Patricia Kite; illustrated by Anca Hariton.
p.   cm.
Summary: Follows seven dandelion seed parachutes which the wind
blows into the air and which land in different circumstances
as an example of the way in which a common plant regenerates.
ISBN 0-7613-0037-6 (lib. bdg.) ISBN 0-7613-0377-4 (pbk.)
1. Dandelions—Juvenile literature. 2. Seeds—Dispersal—Juvenile literature.
[1. Dandelions. 2. Seeds—Dispersal.] I. Hariton, Anca, ill. II. Title.
QK495.C74K48 1998
583'.99—dc21 97-11827 CIP AC

Published by The Millbrook Press, Inc.
2 Old New Milford Road
Brookfield, CT 06804

The spring wind blows.

Seven dandelion seed parachutes fly into the air.
The seed parachutes are made of tiny soft hairs.
Where will each seed parachute land?

The first seed parachute lands in a garden.
Dandelion seed parachutes have tiny hooks
that help them stay in a landing place.

A thick root grows. Green leaves appear.

A gardener sees the dandelion.

"Out, weed," the gardener says.

But the dandelion grows back from a piece
of root the gardener leaves behind.

The second seed parachute lands in a sidewalk crack.
The earth there is hard and dry. The seed lies there
for two years. But after one rainy winter, it starts to grow.

People step on the leaves, but they grow anyway.

The third seed parachute lands in a park. A bird sees the seed. It eats the seed and looks for another.

The fourth seed parachute lands near a forest. Leaves grow.
Deer come and eat all the green leaves. But new leaves
keep coming up from the strong root they leave behind.

The fifth seed parachute lands in a stream.

It floats away, and later the seed grows
on a muddy shore.

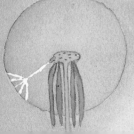

The sixth seed parachute lands on a ship.

The seed goes to a faraway land.

The seventh dandelion seed parachute travels

more than 100 miles on the spring wind.

It lands in

a school yard.

Here the seed grows roots, leaves, stalks, and flowers.

Bees come. They carry pollen from each flower to
their hives. The pollen helps feed young bees.

One day the flowers close up.

When they open, the yellow dandelion is gone.
In its place is a feathery white ball.

A child picks the dandelion.
"Puff!"

Seventy seeds fly into the air.
Where will *they* go?

FACTS ABOUT
DANDELIONS

How did the dandelion get its name?

Dandelion leaves have jagged edges. The French thought the leaves looked like lions' teeth. So they called the plant *dent de lion*, or "lion's tooth." Over the years that name changed, in the English language, to dandelion.

Do dandelions have any other names?

Common American names are blowball, timetable, Irish daisy, and fortune-teller. In China, the dandelion is called "earth nail" because of its long, strong taproot.

The dandelion also has a scientific name: *Taraxacum officinale*. *Taraxacum* comes from the Greek words *taraxos*, meaning "disorder," and *akros*, meaning "remedy." Long ago, people thought that parts of the dandelion helped them become healthy. The word *officinale*, meaning "official," was added to show how important the dandelion was as a medicinal plant.

Where did the dandelion come from?

The dandelion probably got its start in Asia. Nobody is quite certain, as it had spread throughout much of the world before plant histories were written.

But there were no dandelions in North America before the early settlers came from Europe. When settlers sailed from Holland, Germany, France, England, and other countries to North America, the women often brought dandelion seeds with them. Dandelion leaves were used in stews.

Native American Indians, including the Apaches, began using dandelions as part of their food supply, too. The dandelion's seed parachute soon spread the plant all over America.

Is a dandelion one flower or many?

Each dandelion is usually thought of as one flower. But it is really many tiny yellow flowers, or "florets," bunched together on one base.

Do all dandelions have yellow flowers?

There are more than 1,200 different kinds of dandelions. Colors include white, orange, black, and copper.

What is the milky fluid that comes from the stem when a dandelion is picked?

The fluid is called latex. It is also found in the root of the dandelion.

What animals eat dandelions?

Deer, rabbits, moose, woodchucks, elk, bears, mice, and many birds like to eat dandelion seeds or leaves. In city areas, where concrete often covers the ground in which flowers might have grown, pollen from the hardy dandelion feeds bees and keeps them from starving.

Can people eat dandelions?

Early peoples ate all parts of the dandelion. Many people still like new leaves in a salad. (Leaves on older flowering dandelions are very bitter.)

The plant contains vitamins A, B, and C, plus the minerals calcium, sodium, and potassium. It is possible to dry and roast the roots to make a coffee substitute. And some people make dandelion wine.

If you want to experiment with dandelions as food, you should grow your own, free of poison sprays. Some garden dandelions may be sprayed with poison, since gardeners think of them mostly as weeds.

Why don't most gardeners like dandelions?

Most gardeners like all-green lawns. Dandelion leaves grow in a wide circle close to the ground. This leaf mat shuts off air and sunlight from grass growing under it. Dandelions are tougher than grass, and soon the gardener can have a mostly dandelion lawn.

Dandelions are designed for survival. Because of this, they are one of the most common wildflowers. If you try to dig one up and leave even a piece of the large main root, or taproot, the dandelion will soon grow again, unless the root is sliced off close to the bottom.

How long is a dandelion taproot?

A dandelion taproot can be up to three feet (90 centimeters) long. That's longer than your arm!

What are some stories about dandelion parachutes?

Puff three times at a dandelion's full parachute ball. Count the number of individual seed parachutes remaining. This predicts how many children you will have.

Puff three times at a dandelion's full parachute ball. Count the number of individual seed parachutes remaining. This tells you what time it is.

Make a wish and puff on a dandelion's full parachute ball. If all the tiny parachutes fly off, your wish will come true.

ABOUT THE AUTHOR AND ARTIST

Patricia Kite has written about such fascinating creatures as sea slugs, jellyfish, and crabs in her previous books for young readers. Her most recent title is *Insect-Eating Plants*.

She holds a teaching credential in biology and a master's degree in journalism, and her articles on carnivorous plants have appeared in *Flower and Garden* and other publications. She lives in Newark, California.

Anca Hariton was trained as an architect at the University of Bucharest, a profession that she is still involved with when she is not illustrating children's books. She has illustrated *Egg Story*, *Butterfly Story* and, most recently, *Compost! Growing Gardens From Your Garbage* by Linda Glaser. All three science books were named Outstanding Science Trade Books for Children by the National Science Teachers Association/ Children's Book Council.

A resident of Richmond, California, Anca has lots of pets, one of which is a tortoise that likes to nibble on dandelion leaves.